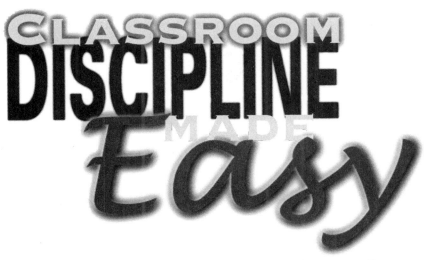

CLASSROOM DISCIPLINE MADE Easy

A Guide for Christian Teachers

BARBARA BOLTON

The Standard Publishing Company, Cincinnati, Ohio
A division of Standex International Corporation
Text © 1997 by Barbara Bolton
All rights reserved
Printed in the United States of America

Cover design by SETTINGPACE
Cover illustration by Joe Stites. © 1997 The Standard Publishing Company

04 03 02 01 00 99 98 97   5 4 3 2 1

ISBN 0-7847-0579-8

Contents

4 **An Ounce of Prevention . . .** **35**

5 **"OK, I've Tried All of Your Suggestions. But They Still Act Up!"** **55**

Preface

In 2 Timothy 4:2 we are instructed to "Preach the Word; be prepared in season and out of season; correct, rebuke and encourage—with great patience and careful instruction." That's a lot of responsibility, particularly for those of us who are teachers. Let's read it again: correct, rebuke, and encourage—with patience and careful instruction.

We are more than disseminators of information. We shape children's lives. We teach the kids the three R's—reading, 'riting, and 'rithmetic. We teach them songs like "Jesus Loves Me"; stories about David and Goliath; and promises, such as "Everyone who calls on the name of the Lord will be saved." But just as important are the lessons on sharing, caring, loving, and respecting—lessons we teach through discipline.

Discipline has many benefits:

- Calm, pleasant learners who are beginning to develop self-discipline.

- A classroom atmosphere that fosters effective learning.

- Behavior patterns that are pleasing to God.

- A classroom with a loving, caring atmosphere.

- A safe environment.

- Positive relationships between teacher and pupils.

- Positive relationships among learners.

- A sense of excitement about learning.

- Learners whose needs are being met.

Proverbs 1:2-4, 7 underscores the importance of self-discipline: "for attaining wisdom and discipline; for understanding words of insight; for acquiring a disciplined and prudent life, doing what is right and just and fair; for giving prudence to the simple, knowledge and discretion to the young . . . The fear of the Lord is the beginning of knowledge, but fools despise wisdom and discipline." Don't let the task of discipline overwhelm you. Take it a step at a time, a day at a time,

"The fear of the Lord is the beginning of knowledge, but fools despise wisdom and discipline."

—Proverbs 1:7

and with a prayerful attitude. You will soon be blessed by see-
ing your learners develop attitudes and habits that will help
them bring honor and glory to God.

Discipline—

one OF THE MOST

loving

THINGS YOU CAN DO FOR

a child

"For snack time I gave them sugar cane and cola."

Discipline is frequently defined as training that uses a blend of rewards and punishment to influence behavior. It maintains a delicate balance between affirmation and punishment. A primary goal is to help people want to act in ways that are acceptable.

Development of self-discipline is the ultimate goal.

Children in particular need guidance as they prepare for and grow toward adulthood. As we teach them at home, at church, and at school, we try to point them toward attitudes and behaviors that will benefit not only them, but classrooms and families as well.

When children come together as a group, behavior challenges frequently arise. Children naturally think of what they would like to do, what they would like to see happen, what is most enjoyable for them. They don't spend a lot of time thinking about what is best for the group. Developing self-discipline—or being aware of what is best for the greatest number of people in the group—is a gradual process. Effective learning does not occur in chaos. There must be some order and sense of well-being for learners to function comfortably.

Teachers need to approach disruptive behavior positively. Instead of thinking about "discipline problems," consider the term "behavior challenges." Most of us approach a challenge positively and even look forward to it. We enjoy the possibilities of creative approaches that are part of the learning process. The label "discipline problems" causes us to feel negative about the behavior, the classroom setting, and sometimes even the disruptive child. A positive attitude together with well-planned and caring responses will enable our students to value working, playing, and learning together in a

Teachers need to approach disruptive behavior positively.

setting that provides opportunities for enjoyable and meaning-ful learning experiences. Behavior challenges are merely opportunities to positively influence the lives of our learners.

Preventing behavior challenges is our first goal. Section four will offer practical methods for doing so. But before we discuss these methods, we must look at some basic principles of teaching, and their implications for discipline. Section five will provide some practical actions to take when we are faced with behavior challenges. Section six will suggest specific responses appropriate for a variety of behaviors.

Develop a plan. Work the plan. You will be pleased by the results.

Throughout the ages God has disciplined his people. When he created man, he planned for everything that man needed. He placed Adam and Eve in the garden, and told them not to eat fruit from the tree in the middle of the garden. When Adam and Eve chose to disobey God and eat the fruit, sin entered the world. Punishment followed the sin.

God continues to love us. He loves each of us so much that he provides a way for us to come to him in spite of our sin. He is ready to forgive. Yet he still disciplines us. In Hebrews 12:5, 6 we read, "My son, do not make light of the Lord's discipline, and do not lose heart when he rebukes you, because the Lord disciplines those he loves, and he punishes everyone he accepts as a son."

God planned for children to be disciplined. Throughout Scripture parents are instructed to discipline their children. Teachers must discipline as well. As parents and teachers become a team and work together consistently, children will realize the best possible growth experience.

CHAPTER 1

A Biblical Perspective

- Discipline is God-ordained.
- Careful planning and preparation will discourage behavior challenges.

True discipline is a demonstration of love.

Proverbs 23:13 states, "Do not withhold discipline from a child." Train. Love and encourage. Teach well. Model the desired behavior. Affirm. Accept. Plan and prepare well so that learners will be motivated to participate appropriately in your classroom.

Sometimes teachers hesitate to discipline because they are convinced that the child will be unhappy. Perhaps the child will not want to return to church. Perhaps other adults will think we are too strict. Remember, *we are setting realistic guidelines and then consistently enforcing them*. Proverbs 28:23 encourages us: "He who rebukes a man will in the end gain more favor than he who has a flattering tongue." Remember, *we are disciplining in love*. True discipline is a demonstration of love. "Because the Lord disciplines those he loves, as a father the son he delights in." (Proverbs 3:12)

There is indeed a sound biblical basis for developing a plan for discipline in the classroom. Look for specific ways to use the suggestions herein in your classroom.

SECTION 2

Know

Your

STUDENTS

Knowing your students is essential if you are to have any hope of managing behavior in a way that makes learning possible. This section will discuss general age-level characteristics, individual needs and abilities, and learning styles. It concludes by examining the critical aspect of relationship building. Revisit the material at the beginning of each new school year or when children are promoted in church programs.

It is possible to read entire books giving age-level characteristics (see Reference List). Let's briefly touch on some characteristics that influence our learners' behavior.

1. Expect about a one-minute attention span for each year of age. For example, most three-year-olds have a three-minute attention span; nine-year-olds have about nine minutes.

    Implication: Plan for appropriate length for activities and then remember the length of the attention span and change activities.

    Example: Prepare a variety of activities: sing, play a game, talk about pictures, match objects with words and sentences, discuss, pray. Switch activities often with young children.

2. Until the age of six or seven, many children may not do well with activities that require small-muscle development.

CHAPTER 2

Age-Level Characteristics

- Knowing general characteristics about the age group you are teaching will help you form realistic behavior expectations.

Implication: Provide large-muscle activities for young children.

Example: Play a beanbag toss game to reinforce Bible memory rather than a pencil and paper activity.

3. Children learn in different ways.

Implication: Be sure that every learning session provides for all learning styles.

Example: Auditory learners may listen to a Bible story recorded on cassette. Visual learners may look at pictures depicting the story. Tactile learners may take objects related to the story out of a bag or box. Kinesthetic learners may dramatize the story.

4. Some educators have inaccurately generalized that children in grades 1 through 3 are learning to read and children in grade 4 through 6 are reading to learn. This does not apply to many children.

Implication: Be ready to help children read, or better still, provide some activities that do not require reading at all. Find ways to have children work in teams and learn to help each other.

Example: Organize groups of four or five to complete a research activity. Place reluctant and confident readers together. Structure the activity so that some children read and others record, give an oral report, or illustrate the information.

5. Children need to wiggle. God created them to wiggle. When you expect kids to sit still for the duration of your class, you can also expect to have behavior challenges.

"Think, Gladys, think! Was your third-grade class still with you when you went to story time?"

Implication: Change activities and allow time for constructive movement.

Example: Give children responsibility for distributing materials and supplies. Arrange activities all around the classroom and have children move among them. Use masking tape to create a tic-tac-toe grid on the floor. Have students stand in the places rather than play the game with pencil or chalk.

6. In general, until the age of seven or eight, boys have less-refined physical development and small-muscle control than girls.

Implication: Provide learning experiences that do not require boys to always do the same things as girls. Variety and choice will contribute to successful learning experiences for all children.

Example: Allow boys to choose a building-block activity while girls choose to paint. Boys may march and sing while girls play rhythm instruments. Sometimes boys and girls will choose the same activity, but providing a variety is essential.

Knowing general characteristics about the age group you are teaching will help you form realistic behavior expectations. You cannot expect a three-year-old to sit still for a twenty-minute video. The child will want to get up from her seat and find a toy. Normal childhood development should not be misread as disruptive behavior.

Normal childhood development should not be misread as disruptive behavior.

Individual Needs and Abilities

- Children come to your classroom with varying needs and abilities. These needs and abilities may contribute to disruptive behavior.

God created us in his image. Everyone is special to him. That does not mean, however, that we are all alike. We need to recognize that our students come to us with a wide variety of needs. Some are looking for information. Some hope to find an adult who will listen to them. Still others want to spend time in a place that surrounds them with caring love and concern. Some only want to work and play with their friends. The list of needs could go on and on. Just know that each student in your class is unique and special, a valued creation of God. Learn to appreciate the differences, and try to recognize and meet their needs as much as possible.

Some disruptive behavior comes from children's unmet needs. Children whose parents are overworked or overcommitted may have a desperate need to be heard. Children who are dealing with the birth of a sibling may take out their fear and anger on the children sitting beside them. Be sensitive and understanding as you discipline.

In addition to needs, learners also come to your classroom with a wide variety of skills and abilities. They may be part of families that provide verbal interaction and opportunities to explore and learn from new experiences, or they may come from a home that is abusive and dysfunctional. They may be struggling in school or they may have developed skills beyond their years.

Accept the challenge and thank God for the wonderful opportunity you have to minister to these special children. Appreciate and celebrate the unique qualities of each of your learners. Guide each one to grow and learn to his potential.

Appreciate and celebrate the unique qualities of each of your learners.

Learning Styles

There are four broad learning styles: visual, auditory, tactile, and kinesthetic. We will look at each one briefly. The simplified explanations presented here will help you select classroom activities that will provide opportunities for all learning styles.

Frequently we tend to teach using our own learning style. By doing so, we may reach only a few of our learners! Most children learn with a combination of learning styles, but one style dominates. By observing which activities the children in your class favor, you will know which learning styles to use.

Visual Learners

Visual learners respond well to visual stimuli. They need visual clues—lists, charts, maps, objects, directions, etc.—to help them understand and remember. Include color, pictures, bulletin board displays, and other resources in your room.

Auditory Learners

Auditory learners respond best to sound. These kids are able to follow verbal directions without visual clues. They enjoy learning with cassette tapes and music—even the sounds of working together in a classroom are comforting. They will view these as learning sounds, not distracting sounds.

Tactile Learners

Tactile learners enjoy touching and feeling as they learn. They enjoy using modeling clay, reaching into containers, identifying objects, taking objects out of bags, and telling stories. Tracing letters and numbers, and drawing in sand or cornmeal pans can also enhance learning.

Kinesthetic Learners

Kinesthetic learning takes place when the whole child is involved in the activity. Kinesthetic learners enjoy active games, such as musical chairs, hopscotch, and Twister.™ Large-muscle and drama activities are helpful as well.

Knowing which learning styles fit which children will help you plan your lesson and discipline appropriately.

By observing which activities the children in your class favor, you will know which learning styles to use.

Building Relationships

- Investing time in your students' lives can ward off behavior challenges.

Relationships between teacher and learner as well as relationships among learners are extremely important in providing meaningful learning experiences. Strong relationships are at the heart of developing a loving, caring atmosphere that will minimize behavior challenges.

Simply talking with a child may be the foundation of a positive relationship. Many children do not experience active listening from a significant adult in their lives. Ask questions that will help you know each child individually. You may do this one-on-one as your students enter the classroom, or you may engage several children in conversation. Time on the playground, in the lunch room, or at a church picnic can provide a relaxed opportunity to get to know your kids. I've included a list of questions you may want to ask the children. Give your response to the questions, too. It is important for your students to know you.

1. Who is in your family? (Be sensitive to children who may not live with both parents. Also, a child may list as family members significant people in their lives, even if they aren't blood relatives.)

2. If you could choose a pet for your family, what would it be? Why?

3. If you could do anything you wanted to do inside your house, what would you do?

4. If you could do anything you wanted to do outside your house, what would you do?

5. What makes you feel happy? Sad? Afraid?

6. What game do you like to play?

7. Tell me about one of your friends. What makes a good friend?

8. What do you like best about school?

9. Why do we need to obey rules?

10. What is the best gift you have ever given to someone?

11. What is the best gift you have ever received?

12. What part of the day do you like best?

13. What is your favorite color?

14. What is your favorite food? (You may want to bring bite-size tastes of your favorite foods to share.)

15. If you could go anywhere in the world for a vacation, what place would you choose?

16. What will be the best thing about growing up?

17. What are some things you would like for me to pray about?

18. How would you change our class?

19. What things do you do very well?

20. What things are sometimes hard for you to do?

Resist the temptation to ask twenty questions as though you were searching for information. The questions certainly would not be asked at any one time. Also, avoid questions that only elicit yes/no responses. Your goal is to become better acquainted with these very special children and to allow them to know each other and you, their teacher. Get to the place where casual, comfortable conversation is a part of most class sessions.

Spending time with students outside your classroom nourishes strong positive relationships. The event itself needs to be simple. Consider some of these options:

- Share a picnic lunch together with two or three of your students.

- Host a picnic lunch after church for the children and their families.

- Visit open house at your students' schools.

- Plan an open house after church one Sunday.

Spending time with students outside your classroom nourishes strong positive relationships.

- Sit together during the worship service.

- Stop by a learner's home to take a forgotten coat.

- Occasionally call your students during the week to encourage them.

- Participate in a field trip to the zoo or museum.

- Work together to complete a service project (pull weeds, rake leaves, shovel snow, wash cars, wash windows, visit nursing homes to visit and sing for the guests).

- Bake cookies for shut-ins.

- Send gifts to missionary families who have children the same ages as your learners.

- Wash toys, put puzzles together, etc. for younger children's Sunday school classes.

- Stuff bulletins, sharpen pencils for the backs of pews, deliver doorknob invitations, etc.

Let's see . . . "Insert slot A of part 22 into Jerusalem Temple plate 11
so that tab AB does not cross tab CD. Give a half twist to corner X, carefully placing
Temple Wall Q into slot C . . . ." Uh—who wants to make finger puppets?

Again, the possibilities are endless. Working, playing, and just being together build the kind of relationships that prevent behavior challenges and create an atmosphere in which meaningful learning occurs happily.

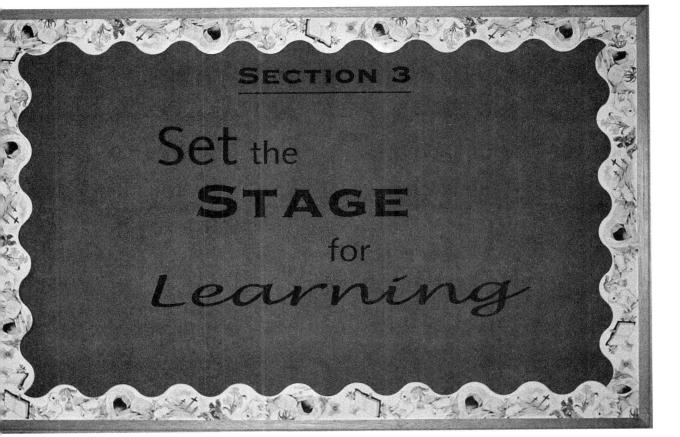

SECTION 3

Set the
STAGE
for
Learning

The learning environment is one influence on children's classroom behavior. We need to consider both the physical and emotional environments, as well as established guidelines for behavior.

We often feel limited by our physical facilities. Never give up! We can create a warm, caring, and inviting area for learning. As much as possible arrange the classroom so that it gives several messages as students walk into the room:

1. "The people here care about me." (Teachers are in the room, ready to teach, and eager to greet and talk with every child.)

2. "There is something to do that I will enjoy." (A variety of activities and materials are ready for children to use.)

3. "This is a pleasant place to be." (The room is neat and clean. The lighting and temperature are comfortable. The furniture is an appropriate size for your students.)

4. "This is an exciting place to be." (The room's appearance changes from time to time.)

Note how the physical environment contributes to disruptive behavior. Is Maria scribbling on Peter's sleeve with a

CHAPTER 6

The Physical Environment

- The physical environment may increase the likelihood of disruptive behavior.

marker? Perhaps the markers should have been out of her reach. Is Randy standing instead of sitting to watch the video? Perhaps he's sitting behind a much taller boy. Be willing to reorganize the room, if necessary, to facilitate learning.

© Andrew Toos

"Since you're also his Sunday school teacher, we were hoping that you would take the brunt of changing Bobby's destructive behavior."

Establishing a positive emotional environment is more challenging than creating a physical environment that promotes learning. But it's worth it. Not only will your learners learn more in a positive emotional environment, but their behavior will be more positive as well.

Test yourself on this. Think of a teacher who influenced your life. What came to mind? The content of his lesson or the relationship you shared with him? You probably do remember what he taught you, but your first memory is that of a relationship. Help your students have the same kind of relationship with you by being a relationship builder.

Although their fellow students play a part in the process, you hold the key. Here are some things you can do to establish an emotional "safe place" for your students.

Invest Time Building Relationships With Learners

We talked about this in chapter 5, but this principle deserves to be emphasized again. What can you do to build caring relationships with your students?

CHAPTER
7

The Emotional Environment

- Children need an emotional "safe place" to learn effectively.
- Safe places are created by building relationships with your students.

Not only will your learners learn more in a positive emotional environment, but their behavior will be more positive as well.

- Know your learners' names.

- Speak to every child individually during class in a friendly and respectful way.

- Ask questions (and share information about yourself) that communicate your interest in each child.

- Invite the child—and family, when possible—to sit with you at a soccer game, worship service, potluck dinner, etc.

- Send a note thanking the child for helping, participating, or behaving well during class.

- Make a telephone call just to say, "How's it going?"

- Send a picture postcard when you are out of town.

- Share a newspaper/magazine clipping related to the child's special interest/hobby.

- Visit the students' homes.

- Smile. (A smile helps to say "I'm glad to be here and I'm glad you're here, too.")

- Maintain eye contact.

- Touch appropriately (hand on arm or shoulder, side-to-side hug).

- Listen attentively.

- Meet special needs as you are able.

The possibilities are endless. We need to be the warm, caring people God created us to be. Reach out to your learners in ways that communicate God's love. The joy of teaching and learning in the framework of strong relationships cannot be surpassed!

"Mrs. Hayes, we're still waiting for your class attendance report."

© Andy Robertson/ANDIGRAFIX

Every classroom needs guidelines for behavior. Here are some suggestions for developing them.

1. State guidelines positively.

2. State them simply.

3. Use age-appropriate vocabulary.

4. Have your students help you establish them.

5. Illustrate them.

6. Display them in the classroom.

As you establish guidelines for your particular class, remember two principles of behavior: Learning does not occur with excessive disruptive behavior, and unsafe behavior cannot be permitted. All behavior that will not be permitted must fall into these categories. Guidelines for elementary learners can be stated as follows:

Our classroom must be a place where we can learn.

Guidelines for Behavior

- Learning does not occur with excessive inappropriate behavior.
- Unsafe behavior cannot be permitted.

Our classroom must be a safe place.

The first statement includes all disruptive behavior. Physical and emotional safely are included in the second statement. The words can be simplified for preschoolers.

Be kind.
Be safe.

The stage is set. The teacher is ready. The learners arrive. Let learning begin!

SECTION 4

An
Ounce
of
PREVENTION...

A substantial number of behavior challenges can be prevented! Let's explore six steps to take to prevent these challenges:

1. Plan and prepare prayerfully and thoroughly.

2. Respect and accept each learner.

3. Include all learning styles in the teaching plan.

4. Provide opportunities for learners to make choices.

5. Use age-appropriate behavior guidelines.

6. Be consistent.

As you use these steps, you will soon notice a vast improvement in your students' behavior. You'll find yourself reinforcing positive behavior more than reacting to negative behavior. It is, however, unrealistic to expect that there will never again be a behavior challenge. Responding to disruptive behavior will be explored in sections five and six.

Lack of careful planning is actually a plan to encourage behavior challenges. If we have not planned prayerfully and thoroughly, we cannot give adequate individual attention to our learners. We sometimes encourage boredom. We don't feel confident and secure. Children sense our lack of preparedness and respond to it in a variety of ways. One of these ways may be in the form of disruptive behavior. Let's consider some important elements of good planning and preparation.

Plan Ahead

Time is a valuable commodity. Most teachers have much to do and wish for more time. If time is in short supply at your household, you might want to pick up Cliff Schimmels's book, *The Last-Minute Sunday School Teacher: Preparing Lessons in a Hurry for Students 9 to 90* (see Reference Guide). But the steps outlined in this chapter have served me well as I've prepared and planned my lessons.

Try to devote some time each day to preparation. Surround every step with prayer. Ask God to provide insights

Step 1:
Plan and Prepare

- Adequate planning can help prevent behavior challenges.

Try to devote some time each day to preparation. Surround every step with prayer.

that will help to make the class session meaningful. Pray for learners by name and need, if needs are known. Divide the preparation into five or six steps (bite-size pieces are easier to manage). Here is a possible planning schedule.

- Sunday or Monday—Read Scripture and lesson in curriculum. (Hint: Record Scripture and narrative on a blank cassette. You may be able to listen to it during the week while you're loading the dishwasher, driving to work, cutting grass, folding clothes, etc.)

- Tuesday—Decide which activities to use. Consider children's learning styles. Be realistic in the choice of materials. Consider classroom space. Be sure the activities reinforce Bible content and/or the application of Bible content.

- Wednesday—Complete a written lesson plan—one that works for you. You may choose to begin this earlier in the week and add to it as your planning progresses. I find it helpful to estimate the time needed for each section of the session. List materials needed so that they can be checked off when they are ready.

- Thursday—Pray, review as needed, and work through the activities.

- Friday—Talk through the lesson and pray.

© Ron Wheeler

- Saturday—Review as needed.

- Sunday—Enjoy a wonderful time with your learners.

If you are a schoolteacher, you may be required to submit written plans by Friday for the next week. Even if this is not a requirement in your school, try it. The plan will need to be adapted as you work through the week, but it is a good start for a successful week at school. Plan a unit at a time if units are appropriate and update the plan as the unit progresses.

Integrate Subjects and Topics Whenever Possible

Integrate and apply your lesson to the students' daily lives. Doing so will reinforce the lesson and help the students prepare for the future.

Ask for Help

Parents and other volunteers are willing to contribute to the education program in schools as well as churches. Survey interested adults. Determine their interests and skills. Know their hobbies and things they enjoy doing. Ask for help on a regular basis. Participation in the education ministries of schools and churches develops ownership. A greater number of adults and in some cases teens make an investment in the lives of children.

Step 2: Respect and Accept

- Respect and accept each learner, but not his disruptive behavior.

In Genesis 1:26, 27 we read "Then God said, 'Let us make man in our image, in our likeness, and let them rule over the fish of the sea and the birds of the air, over the livestock, over all the earth, and over all the creatures that move along the ground.' So God created man in his own image, in the image of God he created him; male and female he created them."

Think about the wonder of being in God's image. Think about his unconditional love for every one of us. God loves and accepts every learner—can we do any less? We need not accept all behavior. Some needs to be corrected and guidance provided to change it. But the child must be loved and accepted. Perhaps the question is, "How do we demonstrate love and acceptance?" Here are some suggestions:

1. Use the children's names when speaking to them.

2. Listen attentively.

3. Remember important things about each child. Talk to them about their interests (their families, hobbies, likes, dislikes, pets, favorite things, etc.).

4. Know that children will be different. Accept and enjoy the differences even though they may contribute to a challenge.

5. Be available when children and their families have special needs.

6. Share yourself.

7. Pray for each child individually and specifically.

8. Demonstrate patience.

9. Give attention to the classroom environment. The classroom communicates love and acceptance.

10. Be consistent and fair.

11. Affirm effort as well as success.

12. Demonstrate an attitude of love. Your attitude is communicated nonverbally as well as verbally.

God loves and accepts every learner—can we do any less?

Remember the words of 1 Corinthians 13:4–7, "Love is patient, love is kind. It does not envy, it does not boast, it is not proud. It is not rude, it is not self-seeking, it is not easily angered, it keeps no record of wrongs. Love does not delight in evil but rejoices with the truth. It always protects, always trusts, always hopes, always perseveres."

In chapter 4 we discussed four basic learning styles: visual, auditory, tactile, and kinesthetic. Provide plenty of opportunities to use all of them. Variety will prevent boredom and will increase interest and excitement. And, most individuals learn using a combination of styles.

Also, don't forget that we learn through all five senses. Frequently classroom experiences include the senses of sight and hearing but ignore the other three. Touching, smelling, and tasting can greatly enrich learning experiences.

Learners respond to organization, but flexibility and variety within the schedule will help to prevent behavior challenges.

Step 3: Include All Learning Styles

- Flexibility and variety within the schedule will help to prevent behavior challenges.

Step 4:
Provide
Opportunities
to Make Choices

- When learners participate eagerly and successfully in activities of their choice, you will have fewer behavior challenges.

Allowing students to make their own choices can prevent disruptive behavior.

Church Settings

In church settings, we frequently begin the learning session by allowing students to select from a variety of activities. As they enter the classroom, we briefly explain their choices and encourage them to choose an activity they would like to do. As they will do so, they will unwittingly choose an activity that allows them to use their dominant learning style. Students will avoid a choice that involves skills they do not possess. A child who struggles with reading will not select an activity that involves reading. She will choose an art activity or perhaps a listening center activity.

Sometimes teachers are able to organize classrooms around learning centers. If the class has an adequate number of teachers, there may be a teacher assigned to each center to reinforce directions and to provide conversation opportunities that will enhance learning.

If it is not possible to provide centers, be sure you offer more than one way to participate in the one or two activities available. For example, elementary children may create a newspaper that reports events during the week before Jesus' death and resurrection. Children who enjoy writing may compose the articles. Others may create the illustrations as an art activity. Others may read Scripture or gather information from other resources. Still others may use a photocopier to make copies to distribute to class members or other classes.

Preschool and kindergarten teachers usually think about seven different kinds of activities: art, books, nature, music, family living, blocks, and games and puzzles.

Elementary teachers (children in grades one through six) usually plan for five different kinds of activities: art, drama, music, written activities (creative writing), and verbal activities.

Many activities combine two or three categories. For example, preparing a mural or frieze involves art, some writing (as descriptions or labels are prepared), and perhaps some verbal activity as a narration is given or recorded on cassette.

Allowing students to make their own choices can prevent disruptive behavior.

If several activities are offered at the same time, ask learners to choose one.

When using a drama activity, music may be used for part of the presentation. Some learners may write a simple script. Some may design costumes and scenery.

If several activities are offered at the same time, ask learners to choose one. If only one activity is offered at a time, be sure there is more than one way to participate in it.

School Settings

In school settings, children are usually accustomed to working in classrooms in which more than one thing is happening at a time even if there is only one teacher in the room.

Frequently the teacher is interacting with a small group of learners and everyone else in the class is working independently. This provides an excellent opportunity for learners to select activities. Sometimes they may be doing follow-up work. Sometimes they are using games, books, or other materials that are available when assignments are completed. In other classrooms, individual learners work on a contract basis: the teacher provides guidance for the tasks that are to be completed, and the learner chooses when and how to do the work.

It is helpful to have available some activities that can be completed independently and some that require teamwork. Children benefit from working in teams of two to four.

In some classrooms teachers provide ways for learners to record activities they complete. Usually there are guidelines for how many children may be in one place participating with any one activity and of course, guidelines for acceptable behavior are clear.

Providing adequate directions for activities that learners complete while the teacher is working with others is important. They usually

"OK, listen up, everybody!
Whoever's good in class today gets a free one of these!"

need to be both visual and auditory. Use a chart, transparency, or instruction sheet for the visual learner. Provide an auditory cassette with recorded directions for children to use instead of interrupting the teacher with questions. Designate children to be "direction helpers." Every class will have some children who remember and follow directions easily. They can become helpers during those times the teacher needs to work with an individual or small group.

Provide a meaningful variety of choices and enjoy the excitement that will result when learners select activities they enjoy. When learners participate eagerly and successfully with activities of their choice, you will have few behavior challenges.

Realistic expectations help prevent behavior challenges. Expect behavior that is possible for the children to achieve. Remember that in general, about one minute of attention can be expected for each year of age. Some children can give attention for longer periods of time if they are involved, interested, and motivated. Others will need to wiggle and change activities often.

Consider children's physical development. Each one will be at a unique stage. Some may need to participate in activities using large muscles while others will have developed small muscle control. Many will need to change physical position frequently. Plan for sitting, standing, walking, etc. Use the need for motion constructively by providing games or music. Encourage children to move around without disturbing others who may be sitting quietly. Model acceptance of differences. Encourage thoughtfulness and consideration. Children will respond in ways they observe and experience adults responding to similar situations.

Step 5: Use Age-Appropriate Guidelines

- Expect behavior that the children can achieve.
- Respect and consider your students' differences.

Realistic expectations help prevent behavior challenges.

Remember that some children tend to be quiet and do not communicate verbally with ease. This is especially true when a child joins a group for the first time. Respect their need for privacy, but encourage nonthreatening participation.

Do you remember times you have felt inadequate, frightened, insecure, or uncertain? What kind of response helped you to feel comfortable? Quiet encouragement without force is often the most effective strategy.

Some children are very outgoing and tend to monopolize discussions. Assure them that you appreciate their willingness to participate and you value their contribution, but emphasize that it is important to give everyone an opportunity to be heard.

Generous measures of patience, acceptance, and encouragement coupled with a desire to create a comfortable environment based on students' stages of development, needs, and abilities will help to ensure meaningful learning experiences with a minimum of behavior challenges!

It is so difficult to remain consistent. "Always" and "never" are words that are difficult to maintain. However, learners expect consistency and respond positively when they know they can count on plans and guidelines that are consistent and fair. There will be times that we forget or respond impulsively, but we must be reminded and shown that a guideline for behavior is important to follow.

CHAPTER 14

Step 6:
Be Consistent

- Behavior guidelines must be enforced consistently.

SECTION 5

"OK, I've TRIED All of your Suggestions, BUT THEY Still ACT UP!"

Discipline demonstrates love, and has a goal to develop character and acceptable behavior.

Try as you might to prevent disruptive behavior, from time to time the children will challenge you. Be assured that you are not the only teacher who is called to discipline.

Proverbs 22:6, "Train a child in the way he should go, and when he is old he will not turn from it," is oft-quoted. There is no doubt that discipline is a biblical principle. Yet some people read this verse and equate discipline with punishment. The Bible distinguishes between discipline and punishment. Discipline demonstrates love, and has a goal to develop character and acceptable behavior. The focus is on training and instruction for the purpose of improvement.

Punishment, however, says, "Your behavior is unacceptable. I will impose punishment (a negative experience) to help you remember to demonstrate acceptable behavior." Our goal is to share God's unconditional love and to help children want to act in ways that are pleasing to him. Punishment establishes firm control imposed by the teacher. Discipline implies a team effort—parents and teachers working together to encourage children to grow in healthy, beneficial ways.

Ignore behavior that may be slightly disruptive if learning can continue. Behaviors such as wiggling that does not distract other learners, daydreaming that occurs for a short period of time, quiet visiting, and "working" noise when children are cooperating in an activity generally do not inhibit learning.

The question is often asked, "Why would I want to ignore unacceptable behavior?" Frequently, disruptive behavior is a child's effort to say, "Hey, look at me! I need some attention!" Children learn early on that one of the best ways to get attention from an adult is to interrupt something the adult does not want to have interrupted. We may think that a child is receiving enough attention, but if he feels a need for more, he actively demonstrates his need.

Practice giving attention for positive behaviors rather than disruptive behaviors. Praise and affirm the child who is learning without incident. Give positive attention to the child who acts disruptively before the disruptive behavior occurs.

CHAPTER 15

Ignore Some Behavior

- Ignore behavior that does not inhibit learning.
- Give attention to positive, not negative, behaviors.

CHAPTER 16

Refer to Behavior Guidelines

- The children should be part of developing the behavior guidelines.

Remind children of those few, simply stated guidelines for acceptable behavior. Display them in the room. Children who can read will be reminded with a glance. Younger children can respond to sketches or stick figure drawings. At the very least, adults in the room will be reminded of the guidelines that have been established.

Those simple guidelines will help you respond to disruptive behavior in positive ways that will encourage learners to demonstrate acceptable behavior. Choose phrases or questions that quickly remind learners of the expected actions:

- "Justin, remember we are going to act in kind ways."

- "Joel, what can you do to help Jonathan?"

- "Benjamin, how can you help us learn just now?"

- "Ashley, show us the words that say 'Be safe!'"

- "Sarah, what can you do to be safe?"

- "Thanks for helping Jared, Micah."

- "Kayley, what will you do to be kind to Alesiah?"

- "Chelsey and Brittani, working together is a one way to help us learn in our classroom."

With each new group of children, work together to word the guidelines for acceptable behavior. As new children become part of the class, review the guidelines. Change them as needed. Refer to them as often as necessary.

If you get discouraged, remember what Hebrews 12:11 says: "No discipline seems pleasant at the time, but painful [even for those doing the disciplining]. Later on, however, it produces a harvest of righteousness and peace for those who have been trained by it."

"No discipline seems pleasant at the time, but painful. Later on, however, it produces a harvest of righteousness and peace for those who have been trained by it."

—Hebrews 12:11

CHAPTER 17

Discipline Individually

- Discipline the child privately, when possible.
- Be sure the child can identify the inappropriate behavior.

We never want to embarrass or ridicule children in any way. If we discuss their behavior in front of the entire class, or a small group of children, or even one other child, we risk negative responses among the children.

Interact one-on-one with a child who has behaved in a disruptive or thoughtless way. This may be difficult if you are the only adult present. Deal with the behavior immediately—particularly if it is unsafe—but be as quick and unobtrusive as possible. Then soon after the incident, follow up with the child and turn the episode into a positive experience.

Frequently children cannot tell us why they acted as they did. It is important, however, that they do identify the inappropriate behavior. If they cannot do so, you should so that both of you will know what your conversation is about. It is not necessary for children to verbalize why they behaved disruptively.

Children may exhibit unacceptable behavior because they do not know or they may have forgotten the guidelines. Perhaps they are testing the boundaries or demonstrating a rebellious spirit. No matter what the cause of their behavior, you need to discuss it briefly with them and come to some conclusion about the next step in the process of developing and demonstrating acceptable actions.

Spear

© Kevin Spear

"See Bobby? This is why we don't allow running in the halls."

Explain Why Behavior Is Unacceptable

- Explain why behavior is inappropriate in simple terms.
- Begin to encourage students to contribute to their classmates' learning experiences.

Simple explanations will help learners understand why a stated behavior is not acceptable. The following are examples of helpful statements.

- "Jenny, I can't let you run in our room. It is not safe. You may fall or bump into someone else and hurt them."

- "Remembering our guidelines is not always easy, Todd. You need to work quietly so that we all can learn."

- "Taking a book from Ian is not a kind thing to do, Jon."

- "Linda, I can't let you play with the balls when everyone else is napping. It would not be kind to disturb their rest."

Simple explanations will help children begin to think about the consequences of their actions. They will begin to consider others' feelings and realize that thoughtless actions do not help the others feel comfortable or learn effectively. Children should be led to have a strong desire to contribute to the learning experiences of their classmates.

Children must accept responsibility for their behavior. When I was a child I tried to explain an act of misbehavior by telling my mother, "The devil made me do it." She responded quickly and with wisdom: "The devil may have tempted you to do it, but no one made you do it. You made the choice to do it."

All of us act impulsively sometimes. Most frequently our behavior—good and bad—is the result of a deliberate choice. We only reap rewards when we make good choices.

Learners Are Responsible for Their Behavior

- Teach children to accept responsibility for their choices—good and bad.

CHAPTER 20

Respond Fairly and Consistently

- Respond to disruptive behavior fairly and consistently.
- Provide logical consequences for disruptive behavior.

Preschoolers are just beginning to experience the consequences of their actions. Their world centers around themselves. They think in terms of "What do I want?" rather than "What would be best for everyone in my class?" These insights are directly related to experience. They are just beginning to understand natural consequences:

- "If I touch a hot stove, I will burn myself."

- "If I play outside in the rain, I will get wet."

- "If I take a toy away from someone, she will cry and will try to get it back."

- "If I cross the street when the light is red, I may be hurt."

- "When I pull on the dog's tail, I may be bitten."

Elementary children understand natural consequences and easily understand that their choices of behavior have logical consequences.

Letting children experience the consequences of their actions is one of the most effective ways to help children accept responsibility for their behavior. Here is one classroom example: "Steve, I can't let you paint on Dana's paper. You may put your name on a clean piece of paper and draw on it, or you may use the puzzles."

Notice that the individual is given opportunity to choose. He can decide to act in an acceptable manner or participate in a different activity. That does not mean that Steve can never again use paint, but he may not paint during this session because he has chosen to misuse materials. The consequence of misusing materials is not using them.

It is important to follow through with the consequence if the undesirable behavior continues after one reminder. Using the statement "If you do that one more time…" only prolongs the misbehavior and encourages children to test the validity of your statement. State the consequence of the behavior and follow through quickly. One reminder is adequate. Be sure the consequence is related to the behavior. For example, the

State the consequence of the behavior and follow through quickly.

"I bought you all a T-shirt."

© David W. Harbaugh

consequence for throwing a block is the loss of the opportunity to use the blocks. The consequence of disrupting the class by distracting conversation with a friend is moving to a place in the room that is not near that particular friend. You may accompany your actions with a statement such as, "I know you like to visit with Kathi, but we cannot learn when you visit too much, so for now, you need to sit here."

Children will respond positively to reinforcement of the guidelines when logical consequences are enforced fairly and consistently. They will begin to develop a desire to function within the guidelines. They will understand that the guidelines apply to everyone. And they will be on the path to "a harvest of righteousness."

What to Do

When...

This section provides a quick reference of sorts, suggestions that will help you deal with students who talk out of turn, disrespect others, are easily distracted, refuse to respect behavior guidelines, and exhibit characteristics of attention deficit disorder (ADD) or attention deficit hyperactivity disorder (ADHD). In many cases, a suggestion is followed by an example of the principle in action.

It is my sincere desire that you will find this list helpful as you point the children in your care to lives filled with hope and promise.

Learners Talk Out of Turn

1. If the talking is not too disruptive, ignore it.

2. Remind the children of the guidelines.

"Remember our rule that says we must be able to learn in our room. We need to talk more quietly. Or, we need to stop talking until we finish reading."

3. Remind the kids that others' opinions are important too.

"Monica, you have good ideas, but we need to hear from two other people before you talk again."

4. Praise them when they correct inappropriate behavior.

"Rick, thank you for waiting for a time to talk when no one else is talking."

5. Catch them doing something right.

"Thanks for working quietly, Jeff."

Praise your students when they correct inappropriate behavior.

6. Gently redirect them to the lesson.

"Donna, it's great fun to visit with our friends, but just now we need to work quietly."

7. Give them one opportunity to correct their behavior and point out the consequence of making the wrong choice.

"If it is too hard for you to work quietly next to Tom, you will need to move to the chair right over here."

8. Allow the talking to continue briefly.

"Let's visit for one minute. I'll watch the clock and let you know when it is time to stop talking."

9. Point them toward a future goal.

"It's just five minutes until lunch. Please work quietly until then."

10. Introduce a different learning style.

"Let's sing a song and then we will work quietly for eight minutes."

Learners Disrespect Others

1. Remind the children of the guidelines.

"Everyone in our room needs to feel safe. That means happy to be here as well as not be hurt."

2. Ask the child to think of a kind way to accomplish her goal.

"Acting in kind ways is important. Ruth, how can you ask Jon for the book without making him feel sad?"

3. Ask them to think of a kind way to accomplish their goal.

"Leticia, our Bible tells us to use kind words. What can you say when you would like for Brian to give you a turn to swing?"

4. Ask them to consider the Golden Rule, "Do unto others...."

"Erica, how do you feel when someone calls you a name? What should you say when you want Jennifer to listen to you?"

5. Ask them to demonstrate respectful behavior.

"Look around the room, Marcy. Show me how you can go from here to the games without upsetting anyone in our class."

6. Restate or clarify the guidelines.

"When our rules chart says, 'Be safe,' it means we act in ways that will not hurt anyone or cause anyone to be sad."

7. Give them one opportunity to correct their behavior and point out the consequences of making the wrong choice.

"Andy, you need to choose to treat everyone in the room thoughtfully or work by yourself."

8. Point out why a behavior is disruptive.

    "Allison, I cannot let you trip people when they walk by your chair. It could cause someone to fall. Everyone in our room needs to be safe."

9. Emphasize that God is not pleased by disruptive behavior.

    "God loves everyone. Each one of us is special to him. Mark, you may not be rude to others when they do not play baseball as well as you do. You may help then learn how to play the game. Or, you may choose something else to do on the playground."

10. Give some responsibility that involves another child to the learner who may be experiencing difficulty with other learners.

Point out why a behavior is disruptive.

"Terry, you are an expert memorizer. Please help Josh with the Bible verse game."

Learners Are Easily Distracted

1. Organize the room into learning centers (areas where a variety of activities are used). Plan for adequate space between each one.

2. Provide fewer activities at one time.

3. Experiment with creative room arrangements.

4. Arrange chairs so that learners have their backs to distracting activities.

5. Record directions on blank cassettes so that learners can review directions without distracting other learners or the teacher.

6. Remind learners about the guideline that says, "Our room must be a place where we can learn."

"Mary, it is difficult for us to learn when you are tapping your feet (bumping the table, humming a tune, etc)."

7.   Remember that some distracting behavior is simply accidental and not intended to distract. A gentle reminder is usually quite effective.

8.   Encourage good work and study habits.

9.   Ask learners who are distracting others to move to a place in the room where they can concentrate more easily and will be less likely to be disruptive.

Encourage good work and study habits.

Learners Refuse to Respect Behavior Guidelines

1.   Point out the guideline and remind the student that in order for everyone to be safe—or learn in our classroom—they must remember to act in ways described by the guidelines.

**Identify the
misbehavior and
be sure the
learner knows
why the behavior
will not be
tolerated.**

2. Identify the misbehavior and be sure the learner knows why the behavior will not be tolerated.

3. Make statements and requests that will motivate students to work within the guidelines:

    - *"Too much noise is making it hard for us to learn, Pete. What can you do to help?"*

    - *"Todd, you need to find a place in the room where you can work well."*

    - *"There is a reason for walking in our room. What is it, Tisha?"*

    - *"John, fighting will hurt someone. What is another way to let someone know you are angry?"*

    - *"Jess, what are some good ways to get my attention?"*

4. Be calm, but firm.

5. If refusal to respect behavior guidelines persists, seek assistance. In a school setting, the principal or another teacher may be asked to reinforce the necessity to accept the behavior guidelines. In a church setting, enlist the help of another member of the teaching team. Perhaps a coordinator or staff member can be of assistance. In some extreme cases, temporary removal from the classroom may be advisable. The child must be removed to the care of another adult. Don't just have him stand outside the door. The goal is to help the learner return to the classroom and function with a measure of success.

6. Speak to the child in a position that allows you to have eye contact. Provide some one-on-one attention.

7. Set limits with choices and consequences. Say something like, "You have a choice. Use the clay properly or not at all." If the child continues to misuse the clay, say, "I'm sorry you made that choice. Now you must put it away and choose a book or a game."

Set limits with choices and consequences.

79

8. Children may interpret your lack of response to their misbehavior as approval. So be consistent when enforcing the guidelines.

9. From time to time review the guidelines.

10. Work with learners to revise guidelines as needed. Sometimes they need to be more specific. Working together will help the learners have ownership in the guidelines.

The "always perseveres" at the end of 1 Corinthians 13:7 is an important reminder to us when we are teaching children who have difficulty working within the guidelines.

Learners Exhibit Characteristics of ADD/ADHD

Sometimes children who struggle to function comfortably in the classroom are identified as children with ADD/ADHD. Some of their disruptive behavior is typical for ADD/ADHD children.

Get to know each student so that you can better understand reasons for their behavior. At times, however, the "whys" will not be justifiable and you will have to respond appropriately. Check the Reference Guide for resources that will provide additional information about ADD/ADHD.

Following are some characteristics of ADD/ADHD children. Notice that this list also describes some children who do not have this disorder.

- Unable to focus their attention; easily distracted by everything they see and hear

- Behave impulsively

- Disorganized

- Have poor motor control

- Have short attention spans

- Talk excessively

- Wiggle

You will notice that many of these characteristics are part of the developmental process. Here are some practical things you can do to help a child struggling with these characteristics to function successfully in the classroom.

1. Capture his attention before giving directions.

2. Use eye contact and physical closeness.

3. Maintain a predictable classroom schedule when possible.

4. Color-code activities.

5. Change the pace of activities.

6. Help peers understand, accept, and help a child who may have ADD/ADHD.

7. Establish a "buddy" system with peers. Everyone will benefit from this process.

8. Communicate with the child's parents. They may be able to provide insights that will help their child function successfully.

9. Make sure the guidelines are accompanied by simple sketches.

10. Encourage the child with ADD/ADHD to sit near a calm child.

Thank God for the opportunity to invest in the life of this special child and his family. The church family should be a group that will sincerely support families who may be struggling to help their children become part of a learning group. "I thank my God every time I remember you" (Philippians 1:3).

Learning Styles—Reaching Everyone God Gave You to Teach,
by Marlene D. LeFever. Colorado Springs, CO: David C.
Cook, 1995.

*The Last-Minute Sunday School Teacher: Preparing Lessons
in a Hurry for Students 9 to 90*, by Cliff Schimmels.
Cincinnati, OH: Standard Publishing, 1997.

100 Ideas That Work! Discipline in the Classroom, by
Sharon R. Berry. Colorado Springs, CO: Association of
Christian Schools International, 1994.

Preschool and Kindergarten Discipline, by Ollie E. Gibbs and
Virginia Kennedy. Whittier, CA: Association of Christian
Schools International, 1993.

Tips for Teachers—Early Childhood, compiled by Peggy
DaHarb. Cincinnati, OH: Standard Publishing, 1995.

Tips for Teachers—Elementary, compiled by Diana Golata
and Nancy Karpenske. Cincinnati, OH: Standard
Publishing, 1995.

Reference Guide

You and Your ADD Child, by Paul Warren and Jody Capehart. Nashville, TN: Thomas Nelson, 1995.

The following cartoonists have contributed to this book:

David W. Harbaugh, page 66

Jonny Hawkins, page 49

Dan McGowan, page 23

Steve Phelps, pages 2 and 11

Andy Robertson/ANDIGRAFIX, page 32

Kevin Spear, page 61

Andrew Toos, page 28

Ron Wheeler, page 39